# WORSHIP *at* HOME

## LENT 2021

## A Season of Promise

# Other Resources for Worship and Preaching

*Abingdon Worship Annual*
edited by Mary Scifres and B. J. Beu

*Abingdon Preaching Annual*
edited by Charley Reeb

*Prepare! An Ecumenical Music and Worship Planner*
by Mary Scifres and David Bone

*The United Methodist Music and Worship Planner*
by Mary Scifres and David Bone

Find a rich collection of free and subscription resources for weekly
worship and preaching at ministrymatters.com/worship.

LENT 2021

# WORSHIP
## *at* HOME

### MARY SCIFRES
### AND BJ BEU

Abingdon Press™
*Nashville, TN*

WORSHIP AT HOME:
LENT 2021

*Copyright © 2021 by Mary Scifres & B. J. Beu*

All rights reserved.

No part of this work may be reproduced or transmitted in any form or by any means, electronic or me-
chanical, including photocopying and recording, or by any information storage or retrieval system, except
as may be expressly permitted by the 1976 Copyright Act or in writing from the publisher. Requests for
permission should be addressed in writing to Permissions, Abingdon Press, 2222 Rosa L. Parks Blvd.,
Nashville, TN 37228-1306, or permissions@abingdonpress.com.

ISBN: 9781791019037

Scripture quotations unless noted otherwise are from the Common English Bible. Copyright © 2011 by
the Common English Bible. All rights reserved. Used by permission. www.CommonEnglishBible.com.

Scripture quotations marked (NIV) are taken from the Holy Bible, New International Version ®, NIV®.
Copyright © 1973, 1978, 1984, 2011 by Biblica, Inc.™ Used by permission of Zondervan. All rights
reserved worldwide. www.zondervan.com. The "NIV" and "New International Version" are trademarks
registered in the United States Patent and Trademark Office by Biblica, Inc.™

21 22 23 24 25 26 27 28 29 30—10 9 8 7 6 5 4 3 2 1
MANUFACTURED IN THE UNITED STATES OF AMERICA

# CONTENTS

# CONTENTS

# INTRODUCTION

Last year, most of us experienced an abrupt interruption to our Lenten journey when the global pandemic reached American shores. This Lenten journey is likely to feel just as strange as we move toward Easter unsure of whether and when we can gather together for in-person worship. How do we craft a sacred season amidst so many unanswered questions? How can we embrace the gift of being at home with joy, while also facing our sorrows and fears about events and people we are missing? Wherever you are on this journey, this book is our gift to you. In these pages you will find resources to create and claim new traditions and rituals for yourself and your loved ones. Even if you have the opportunity to gather for live worship with a faith community or are leading others in worship through this sacred season, you will find here words, songs, rituals, and activities to help map a personalized spiritual journey through Lent. Use these services for communal worship with family and friends, or for personal devotion and spiritual growth. You may even use these resources to enhance live and large-group gatherings.

As you read and utilize this second volume in the *Worship at Home* series, we welcome your feedback and invite you to email us with ideas on how to shape this resource to best fit your needs. You will find our contact information, along with a free offer, at the end of this introduction. To explore how to use this resource as an individual, a family, a pastor, or a congregation, read the following chapter, "How to Use This Book."

# The Gift of Journeying through Lent at Home

Worship as we know it today is a modern phenomenon. Even as Christians began building structures to hold worship in the fourth century, worship continued in homes and neighborhood buildings, with only occasional pilgrimages to cathedrals and basilicas. In the earliest days of Christendom, novitiates to the faith would study for two years in preparation for their Easter baptism. Lent was the final step on that lengthy journey, but still it was a journey most often traveled in homes, catacombs, and neighborhood gathering places. We invite you to embrace this idea of the Lenten season as a time for journeying toward Easter personally or corporately, privately or publicly, intimately with a few close friends and family members or socially with a larger church community.

We invite you to create your own Lenten traditions, adapting the ideas we offer into worship services and words that nurture and inspire you, your family, and your faith community. Here, you will find an invitation to return to the quieter, introspective aspects of this season. Read the words and prayers silently or aloud, sing or listen to the suggested songs, reflect on the meaning of the song lyrics and the wisdom of the scriptures and stories, and participate in the activities and rituals that help you walk with Christ as you prepare to face his death on Good Friday. Share this book with a spouse, a child, a life partner, a friend, your family, a small group, or even neighborhood friends. (Share these services via video conference if need be.) Whether through the valley of the shadow of death or beside still waters, Jesus will travel this journey with you. We hope you will find inspiration and ideas in these pages to strengthen your spirit and sustain your soul.

Yours on the Journey,
Mary Scifres & B. J. Beu

Contact us at admin@maryscifres.com or learn more about us at www.maryscifres.com.

**Special Offer: Free Ebook**
"Transformation: The Heart of the Journey," an excerpt and study guide from Mary's book, *The Gospel According to Beauty and the Beast*, a great conversation starter for Lenten study groups, book groups, or personal reflection:
https://MaryScifres.simplero.com/lentbook

# HOW TO USE THIS BOOK

## Getting Ready

We invite you to read each worship service beforehand and decide how to best use the resources they contain. Choose the activities, words, and songs that fit your preferences and your traditions. Mark up the book if you want, reminding yourself which activities and songs you have chosen. When you are ready to worship, you can do so in several ways. Having previously chosen your song and response options, you can follow the order of service as written. Alternately, you can select a few worship elements to create a brief time of devotion. Another option is to spread out any or all of the worship elements during the week. Many people choose to repeat a meaningful part of the service, like lighting the Christ candle, every day of the week, not just on Sunday. The more you prepare for your Lenten worship experience, the more meaningful your Lenten journey will be. See our list of recommended **Things to Gather Before Lent Begins** at the end of this article.

This edition of *Worship at Home* focuses on God's promises amidst the covenant history of God's people. This tour through salvation history culminates in the gift of Christ Jesus in our world and in our lives. In honor of this gift, we encourage you to light a Christ candle each week as a part of your worship experience. Any candle will do, although traditionally the Christ candle is white. For safety and ease of use, battery-powered candles may be preferable, particularly when worshiping alone or with young children.

During the Lenten season, we invite you to create a *sacred space/worship altar* or your own personalized art project by drawing, painting, sculpting, or gathering one item each week that symbolizes the week's theme. You may even use the symbol to help you reflect on and remember commitments you are making to yourself and to God on your Lenten journey. This is not an activity to over-think. Invite your analytical left brain to quiet down long enough to allow the creative side of your right brain to express truths only accessible through art and imagination. And make sure you leave enough space to add a new item each week to your sacred creation.

Some of the services' Sending Activities also suggest doing a craft or providing a gift to neighbors or strangers. Reading through the activities before Lent will give you time to order craft supplies or gifts beforehand. You don't need to purchase a thing to worship at home during Lent, but if an idea captures your fancy, you will have time to prepare.

## Ideas for Individuals and Families

Home-based worship allows you to tailor certain worship elements to fit your preferences. Think through and make decisions to create what will be most meaningful for you and those worshiping with you. Do you enjoy singing hymns, or do you prefer silently allowing the music to wash over you? Do you prefer instrumental or vocal arrangements? Do you like to discuss scripture, or do you prefer to reflect quietly? Do you want to memorize a scripture verse each week, or do you simply prefer to read, reflect, and move on? Do you like scripture to inspire you into action?

How might this resource help you connect with others? If there are children in your home or church, how might you include them? Might you want to invite a friend or neighbor or grandchild to participate virtually with you in one of the activities or even a full worship service? We hope you will include others and adapt these ideas for whatever is best for your setting.

## How to Use This Resource in Congregational Worship

Although written with individuals, families, and home-based worship in mind, this book also provides excellent resources for pastors and churches yearning for new ways of creating worship together. This resource can help congregations stay connected even while worshiping from home.

It can help pastors and church leaders provide a structured worship order just as written here, but it is easily adaptable for use in a variety of settings during the Lenten season. Many church leaders will use this book as their Sunday morning worship plan. Others may use it to add vespers or morning prayer services throughout the season. Some may lift a few segments for use in youth group gatherings or in other small group worship experiences and discussions. We invite you to use this resource in a way that best serves you and your congregation.

When leading a congregation or group with this worship resource, you can advise your people to collect the appropriate supplies they will need beforehand. Or you may choose to purchase the supplies, as your budget allows, and deliver them to those who will be worshiping from home. While some churches have delivered hymnals to church members worshiping at home, we've eliminated this need by choosing hymns that are readily available online.

## Worship Elements

**Song** selections often have multiple options. If you have a hymnal or songbook of carols, you can open to the song and sing along. You can also consult the index or table of contents of your favorite hymnal and find most songs listed alphabetically by the song's title or first line. If you like to sing along but don't have a hymnal, we've referenced YouTube options, some that include lyrics. If you don't care to sing, you can simply enjoy the music in the videos, which are often set to stunning background imagery.

**Memory Verses** are new with this volume. These short readings invite you to engage beloved and familiar scriptures that may inspire regular recitation. When memorizing with children or older adults, you may shorten the verses to keep the memory work manageable. This exercise should feel life-giving, not challenging. If memory work isn't for you, consider highlighting the verse in your Bible or writing the scripture down and keeping it in a familiar place. Choose the method that best serves your spiritual journey.

**Scripture Readings** may be read by one person or divided up into parts for multiple readers. **Responses to the Word** on Ash Wednesday and Holy Thursday include rituals specific for these days. On other weeks, options are often provided to account for differences in personal preference.

Finally, there are a multitude of **Sending Activities** to help you put your faith into action and connect with others throughout the week. You may choose to focus on one or several each week. Feel free to mix it up week to week. Some of you may even want to see how many activities you can do throughout the week to keep the meaning of the season before you each day. This is a resource for *you.* Use it in the way that best strengthens your faith during this Lenten season.

# Introducing Other Resources

As we designed this book, we searched for other artists to inspire our work and your worship. We are thrilled to introduce you to the groundbreaking work of Cláudio Carvalhaes, Associate Professor of Worship at Union Theological Seminary and a new Abingdon Press author. Cláudio has worked and studied with people around the globe and helped them tell their stories of oppression, pain, and hope through prayers, litanies, and blessings. In *Liturgies from Below: Praying with People at the Ends of the World,* Cláudio offers their words to the world and invites us into their experiences.

We are also honored to share with you a poem by Tina Datsko de Sánchez, poet-in-residence at First Congregational Church of Long Beach, California. Inspired by the poetry of Rumi and Hafiz, Tina's book *Swimming in God: Thirty-One Days of Longing, Thirty Days of Joy, Thirty-One Days of Love* by Pilgrim Press is the first in a four-book series of interfaith spiritual poetry.

# Create a Worship Space in Your Home

Creating a sacred space in which to worship requires intentionality, planning, and effort. Ideally, this is a space that can remain set up throughout the Lenten season. For this volume of *Worship at Home,* we suggest an artistic way for you to add to this sacred space as a part of each week's worship service. Although listed as Sending Activities, you may choose to begin your time of worship by adding the new symbol to your sacred space each week. If you already have a centering or meditation space, use that. If not, pay attention to your body. Find a place that feels open and comfortable. If the space makes your body feel cramped or closed off, your spirit will have a difficult time opening up to the holy. Whether we are physical beings having spiritual experiences or spiritual beings having physical experiences, the result is the same—our bodies, minds, and spirits are intertwined and influence each other. Once you find a space that feels right, you may want to set up an altar on a small table. Swathe the altar with a fabric covering. We use a prayer shawl that was knitted for B. J. when he was undergoing cancer treatment. Decorate your altar with a cross or other sacred objects. These objects can be literally anything that help you feel grounded in God's love and acceptance or that connect you to a sense of the holy. If you wish to participate in the Sending Activity of creating and adding to your sacred space, leave adequate room for additional objects each week. Since each of these worship services recommends YouTube videos, be sure you have a smartphone, tablet, computer, or smart TV with the YouTube app in the room with good access to the internet. Once you are finished, dedicate the space to God. Thank God for meeting you in this place and for being with you during your Lenten journey.

## Things to Gather before Lent Begins

Before Lent begins, take a moment to gather some of these items to enhance your worship experiences.

- A dedicated worship space with smart phone, tablet, computer, or smart TV with the YouTube app (and good internet access)

- A Christ candle and matches, lighter, or batteries (if using an electric candle)

- Print copies of the day's worship service, or access to the ebook on your tablet, phone, or computer

- Piano and hymnal if you prefer to play and sing

- A journal or notepad if you like to write reflections down

- Art or craft supplies (or the symbolic objects you have selected) to add to your art project or sacred space each week

- Art, craft or gift supplies, notecards, Post-it notes, and blank paper for selected Sending Activities

- Blank paper, pen or pencil, ceramic bowl, and matches or lighter to create ashes for Ash Wednesday

- Plate, cup, juice or water, and bread or crackers for Holy Thursday

# CHAPTER 1
# ASH WEDNESDAY: FROM DUST TO PROMISE

## Gathering Music: "Better Than a Hallelujah"

Amy Grant
https://www.facebook.com/amygrant/videos/387443138898470

## Centering Words

The day of the LORD is near—a day of dread and despair. Yet even now, who knows if God will relent and turn our calamity into joy? Leave behind the dust of death and return to God with all your heart.

## Lighting the Christ Candle

*As you light the Christ candle on your altar, focus on the coming Lenten season. Invite the light of Christ to lift you from the dust of death, that you may have both the courage to face your shortcomings, and the strength to nurture your gifts and talents in service of the world.*

## Memory Verse: Psalm 51:10

Create a clean heart for me, God;
  put a new, faithful spirit deep inside me.

## Opening Prayer

Lead me from the dust of death, O God,
  in your mercy and your grace.
Clean my heart with your refiner's fire,
  and put a willing spirit within me,
    for I cannot endure this journey alone.
Bless me with discernment and wisdom,
  and anoint me with patience and perseverance
    as I travel with Christ on the road to the cross.
Amen.

## Song: "Sunday's Palms Are Wednesday's Ashes"

FUMC Pittfield vocalists, percussion, piano, and lyrics
https://youtu.be/FVfgxEBA_oo

## Scripture Reading: Psalm 51:1, 10-11; Joel 2:12-13

Have mercy on me, God,
  according to your faithful love!
Wipe away my wrongdoings
  according to your great compassion!
Create a clean heart for me, God;
  put a new, faithful spirit deep inside me.
Please don't throw me out of your presence;
  please don't take your holy spirit away from me.
Yet even now, says the LORD,
  return to me with all your hearts,
    with fasting, with weeping, and with sorrow;
  tear your hearts and not your clothing.

2

Return to the LORD your God,
>    for he is merciful and compassionate,
>    very patient, full of faithful love,
>        and ready to forgive.

# Meditation

The psalmist calls for a spring cleaning of the heart and soul. Such cleaning cannot be undertaken alone. God is the one who can do this, the one who can put a new and faithful spirit within you. Yet, God cannot do this without your eager consent, or without your willingness to turn a heart of stone into a heart of flesh. Ash Wednesday is a day to tear down the walls of the heart—walls that are built to keep out hurt and pain (but ultimately keep the hurt locked inside), walls that tell God to go away. Ash Wednesday is a day to heed the warning of the prophet Joel and return to the Lord with a full heart, a clean heart—for God's mercy, compassion, and forgiveness are greater than God's anger at human failings.

# Response to the Word: Psalm 22:14-15, Adapted

*Reflect on these words from the psalmist. Read them several times and allow the images to enlighten your mind, fill your heart, and sink into your very bones.*

I'm poured out like water.
My heart is like wax;
>    it melts inside me.
My strength is dried up
>    like a piece of broken pottery.
You've set me down in the dust of death.

# Music for Reflection: "Ashes to Ashes"

Dan Shutte with OCP Music
https://youtu.be/NM1MYet8kNc

# Ritual of Ashes

*Take a small scrap of paper and write down something you would like to give up—something that saps your strength and makes your spirit feel like a piece of broken pottery. Burn the paper in a ceramic bowl until it is reduced to ash. Take a moment to remember that when you turn your burdens over to God, Christ's saving love lifts you from the dust of death through the power of the Holy Spirit. Dip your thumb in the ashes and mark a cross on your forehead or wrist, as a sign of your commitment to be free of this burden. Return to your commitment, this promise you are making to yourself, throughout the season of Lent, that your spirit may be lifted up with Christ on Good Friday. You may keep the remaining bowl of ashes on your altar as a reminder of your commitment throughout the season.*

# Song: "Lord, Who Throughout These Forty Days"

Advent Birmingham ensemble
https://youtu.be/jzqjglKoEpU
*(Note that Stanza 5 has varying lyrics, depending on the hymnal.)*

# Blessing

Tear your heart, not your clothing.
Love with a clean heart.
Walk in the strength of a faithful spirit.
From the dust of death,
    receive from God the promise of new life.

# Sending Activities

*Choose an activity or find your own way to express your Ash Wednesday commitment in the week ahead.*

- Begin the creation of a sacred space/worship altar or art project for the Lenten season by drawing, painting, sculpting, or gathering one item that symbolizes the commitment you are making to yourself and God. Leave enough room to add a new item each week to your sacred creation.

- With children, choose a heart craft project that you can do together or "side by side" on FaceTime or Zoom. As you craft your heart, work on this week's memory verse or talk about how God has changed your heart over the years.

- Send a note of apology to someone you may have hurt or wronged. When you mail the letter, breathe in the peace of letting go, of forgiving yourself.

- Journal or write a note to yourself to embrace the grace and forgiveness you need to allow past regrets to fall away. Then allow God's promises of love and hope to fill you this Lenten season.

- Invite a friend, church group, or family members to video conference with you as you contemplate the meaning of this day. Show one another the ashes on your foreheads, then reflect silently together, using the share screen feature to listen to one of the music videos recommended above.

- Recite today's memory verse each day this week. Use whichever memory technique works best for you: memorize small phrases at a time until you know the entire verse; write the verse on a Post-it note, placing it where you can see and recite it several times each day; imagine a visual for the verse's meaning; or paraphrase the verse and memorize this paraphrase. If memorizing with small children, give them a short phrase before adding additional phrases. Some small children are better at memory work than adults, while others become frustrated if asked to memorize too many words.

# CHAPTER 2
# FIRST SUNDAY IN LENT: RAINBOW PROMISE

## Gathering Music: "Over the Rainbow/Simple Gifts"

Piano Guys piano and cello
https://youtu.be/jzF_y039slk

## Centering Words

After the pouring rain has stopped, after the clapping thunder has stilled, a rainbow bursts forth—God's promise of life to the earth.

## Lighting the Christ Candle

*As you light the Christ candle on your altar, give thanks for the promises of God. Invite the light of Christ to fill you with the joy and beauty of the mist-kissed rainbow covenant God has made with all the creatures of the earth.*

## Memory Verse: Psalm 19:1 NIV

The heavens declare the glory of God;
  the skies proclaim the work of his hands.

## Opening Prayer

Merciful God, you reveal yourself—
  in raging storms and brilliant rainbows,
  in challenging scriptures and hopeful expectations,
  in humble hearts and loving grace.
Guide your servants on this Lenten journey
  from the darkness of death
    to the hope of resurrection. Amen.

## Song: "This Is My Father's World"

Soloist and children's choir with lyrics (from Praise Baby Collection)
https://youtu.be/bEE5MvoT3oI

Fountainview Academy's orchestra and soloist (no lyrics)
https://youtu.be/N3ZVLOLMRMw

Nashville Notes virtual choir (no lyrics)
https://youtu.be/o2OvdvgGthE

# Scripture Reading: Genesis 9:8-11, 13, 16, Adapted

God said to Noah and to his sons with him, "I am now setting up my covenant with you, with your descendants, and with every living being leaving the ark with you—with the birds, with the large animals, and with all the animals of the earth. I will set up my covenant with you so that never again will all life be cut off by floodwaters. There will never again be a flood to destroy the earth. I have placed my bow in the clouds; it will be the symbol of the covenant between me and the earth . . . and upon seeing it I will remember my enduring covenant with every living being of all the earth's creatures."

7

# Meditation

The Lord was so angered by humanity's wicked ways that God decided to start over, sending a flood to wipe out all life save for Noah, his family, and the animals sheltered on the ark. But God appears to regret this drastic decision almost immediately and makes a covenant, not just with Noah and his family, but with all the creatures of the earth to never again destroy all life. The beautiful rainbow God sets as a bow in the clouds serves as a symbol and a reminder of this eternal promise. It is easy to forget God's deep love for all the works of creation. It is easy to judge things as good or bad, right or wrong, solely on the basis of how they affect human beings. It is easy to dishonor God's covenant by failing to care for the planet we live on. Lent is a time to set aside what is easy; it is a time to acknowledge the breadth of God's love for all creation, to receive this amazing promise and to act accordingly.

# Music for Reflection

**"Blessings"**
Laura Story
https://youtu.be/Cd6J6Wgnv4M

–OR–

**"Rainbow"**
Kasey Musgraves
https://youtu.be/6OFv566mj7s

# Response to the Word

*After listening to the Music for Reflection or simply sitting quietly, contemplate where it is raining in your life, your soul, your mind. Are any showers so persistent or overwhelming that they threaten to drown you? Are some showers just soft drizzles that irritate or wear on you, but aren't debilitating? Look at the raindrops and the clouds in your mind; feel the rain upon your face and the clouds darkening your day. Then, imagine a rainbow emerging beneath the clouds and through the raindrops. Envision the colors of the bow emerging, brightening your mind and lightening your mood. Invite God to reveal blessings that might be the "pots of* gold" awaiting you at the end of each rainbow. Draw, sketch, doodle, or write about your experience of this time of reflection and contemplation.

## Song: "In the Midst of New Dimensions"

First-Plymouth Church orchestra and choir with lyrics
https://youtu.be/icJs25Z09ws

Overbrook Quartet and organ with hymnal lyrics
https://youtu.be/LPBp1PWzRzU

Edgewood United Church virtual choir (no lyrics)
https://youtu.be/jMfvYl28qa4

## Blessing

A flood, a boat, and a rainbow promise from God . . .
From the watery grave, God proclaims a covenant of life.

## Closing Music:
## "Somewhere Over the Rainbow"

Judy Garland in *The Wizard of Oz*
https://youtu.be/PSZxmZmBfnU

Israel "IZ" Kamakawiwo'ole
https://youtu.be/V1bFr2SWP1I

Eva Cassidy
https://www.youtube.com/watch?v=2rd8VktT8xY

# Sending Activities

*Choose an activity or find your own way to respond to God's promise in the week ahead.*

- Create or add to your Lenten sacred space/worship altar (or art project) by drawing, painting, sculpting, or gathering one item today that symbolizes God's rainbow promise of hope and life—perhaps a drawing of a rainbow itself.

- With children, choose a rainbow craft you can do together or "side by side" on FaceTime or Zoom. As you craft your rainbow, work on this week's memory verse or discuss how rainbows and God's promises help you persevere through tough times.

- Purchase rainbow postcards or tokens, or draw or print rainbows onto notecards or plain paper. Add a word of hope such as, "Remember that rainbows come after the rain." Deliver your rainbow notes anonymously to neighbors, or send them to people who are sheltering at home alone this month.

- Contemplate your drawing or writing from the Response to the Word from above. Pray for the rain showers in your life to become rainbow blessings in the month ahead.

- If you did not worship on Ash Wednesday, you may still want to do that day's suggested Response to the Word to prepare yourself for the Lenten journey: *Take a small scrap of paper and write down something you would like to give up—something that saps your strength and makes your spirit feel like a piece of broken pottery. Slowly tear the paper up as a sign of your commitment to be free of this burden. Return to your commitment, this promise you are making to yourself, throughout the season of Lent, that your spirit may be lifted up with Christ on Good Friday. You may keep the torn-up paper on your altar as a reminder of your commitment throughout the season.*

- Call a friend and ask if they want to watch a movie of hope and promise "together," either by video conference using "screen share" or simply by sitting in front of a television in your separate homes while talking on the telephone and laughing, crying, and discussing the scenes together. Earbuds can be a big help during long telephone or video calls. Pick a movie you can both easily access, like *Wizard of Oz*, which can be viewed on services like IMDb or Hulu.

- Recite today's memory verse each day this week. Use whichever memory technique works best for you: memorize small phrases at a time until you know the entire verse; write the verse on a Post-it note, placing it where you can see and recite it several times each day; imagine a visual for the verse's meaning; or paraphrase the verse and memorize this paraphrase. If memorizing with small children, give them a short phrase before adding additional phrases. Some small children are better at memory work than adults, while others become frustrated if asked to memorize too many words.

# CHAPTER 3
# SECOND SUNDAY
# IN LENT:
# THE PROMISE OF US

## Gathering Music:
## "The God of Abraham Praise"

Fernando Ortega (instrumental with lyrics)
https://youtu.be/IaYycKwVxQU

## Centering Words

God names you in holy love, claiming you as God's own.

## Lighting the Christ Candle

*As you light the Christ candle on your altar, give thanks for the promise of your place among God's people. Invite the light of Christ to fill you with grace and peace, as you rest in the household of God.*

## Memory Verse: Isaiah 49:6b, Adapted

I will appoint you as light to the nations
    so that my salvation may reach the ends of the earth.

## Song: "The God of Abraham Praise"

Westminster Presbyterian Church's choir, organ, and lyrics
https://youtu.be/kzQbx0LeWOo

Cathedral of St. John the Divine's virtual choir
https://youtu.be/_k0WbiQXiHw

## Opening Prayer

Spirit of the ages, name me and claim me
    according to your purposes.
Train my ear to hear your call,
    and tune my heart to follow your voice.
Raise me as a child of your covenant,
    that I may be an heir of your promise. Amen.

## Children's Moment and Song: "I Am a Promise"

Gaither Music TV's Homecoming Kids
https://youtu.be/DQnJ-mxzZGI

St. Luke Community UMC Children's Choral Anthem
https://youtu.be/_dSUKr3mXys

Fabiola Rosala's singalong version with storybook pictures
https://youtu.be/2dCvSafgCgw

# Scripture Reading: Genesis 17:1-2, 4-15-16 NIV

When Abram was ninety-nine years old, the LORD appeared to him and said, "I am God Almighty; walk before me faithfully and be blameless. Then I will make my covenant between me and you and will greatly increase your numbers. You will be the father of many nations. No longer will you be called Abram; your name will be Abraham, for I have made you a father of many nations. I will make you very fruitful; I will make nations of you, and kings will come from you. I will establish my covenant as an everlasting covenant between me and you and your descendants after you for the generations to come, to be your God and the God of your descendants after you.

God also said to Abraham, "As for Sarai your wife, you are no longer to call her Sarai; her name will be Sarah. I will bless her and will surely give you a son by her. I will bless her so that she will be the mother of nations; kings of peoples will come from her."

# Meditation

Taking the flood as a mulligan in salvation history, it was time for God to start over. Instead of focusing on humanity as a whole, God would work through one family—a family through whom all the peoples of the world would be blessed. If Abram would walk faithfully and blamelessly before the Lord, God would make him a father of nations. God makes this clear by changing Abram's name, which means "exalted father," to Abraham, which means "father of a multitude." Likewise, the name of Abraham's wife will no longer be Sarai, which means "my princess," but Sarah, which makes her a princess on a much broader scale. For Jews, Sarah is considered the mother of every convert to Judaism. For Christians, Sarah is the mother of kings, including King David and Christ Jesus. Abraham and Sarah are chosen by God so that the world might be blessed through them. Later, Isaiah will pick up this theme and call the Israelites to be a light to the nations. The one we walk with on this Lenten journey is heir of this promise and this covenant call—a promise and covenant call you and I share today.

# Music for Reflection:
# "We Are God's People"

Hal Leonard and Shawnee Press choral arrangement
https://youtu.be/3QPymRVOCyU

GRII Bandung's virtual choir with English and Indonesian lyrics
https://youtu.be/wUKmyFC5MfA

# Response to the Word

*Listen to the Music for Reflection or sing the hymn with the virtual choir while contemplating the text. How do you live your calling as one of God's people? What does it mean to "walk heart to heart and hand to hand," particularly in a season when such actions are not as readily available to us? Knowing you are God's promise, called to be a light, how might you and others in your community of faith support one another to "give warmth and light" and inspiration in the weeks and months ahead? Share your commitment with a covenant partner and commit to checking in weekly for the remainder of Lent about your progress. Or write your commitment on a piece of paper and tape the paper to your bathroom mirror so you can check in with yourself each day.*

# Song:
# "God, Whose Love Is Reigning o'er Us"

J. Daniel Ahston's family quartet, with organ and lyrics
https://youtu.be/gB0bJ_C2nY8

OCP Session Choir and Organ (no lyrics)
https://youtu.be/1wjTzFJm_nY

# Closing Prayer:
# A Traditional Prayer from Ghana

"Cover Me with the Night"

Come, Lord, and cover us with the night.
Spread your grace over us,
    as you assured us you would.
Your promises are more
    than all the stars in the sky.
Your mercy is deeper than the night.
Lord it will be cold.
The night comes with its breath of death.
Night comes; the end comes; you come.
Lord, we will wait for you,
    day and night. Amen.

—Cláudio Carvalhaes, *Liturgies from Below:*
*Praying with People at the Ends of the World*
(Nashville: Abingdon Press, 2020)

## Blessing

A calling, a naming, a claiming, and a promise from God . . .
    Once you were not a people, now you are God's people.

## Sending Activities

*Choose an activity or find your own way to express your role as God's*
*promise in the week ahead.*

- Add to your sacred space/worship altar or art project by drawing, painting, sculpting, or gathering an item that symbolizes
  your role as God's promise and as one of God's people to bring
  Christ's light to the world.

- With children, choose a self-portrait craft you can do together or "side by side" on FaceTime or Zoom. You might draw or paint a self-portrait, trace a silhouette, decorate a small mirror, or decorate a wooden person-shaped cutout. Ask curious questions as you work on the art project, getting to know the child(ren) even more fully.

- Deliver small battery-powered votive candles to neighbors, older church members, or friends in need with a note that you are praying they sense God's light surrounding them.

- Light a candle each evening before dinner and pray by name for individuals whom you are worried about, miss, or feel called to help.

- Reflect on an Ash Wednesday or Lenten commitment you made. Is the commitment helping you draw closer to God's people? Why or why not?

- Recite today's memory verse each day this week. Use whichever memory technique works best for you: memorize small phrases at a time until you know the entire verse; write the verse on a Post-it note, placing it where you can see and recite it several times each day; imagine a visual for the verse's meaning; or paraphrase the verse and memorize this paraphrase. If memorizing with small children, give them a short phrase before adding additional phrases. Some small children are better at memory work than adults, while others become frustrated if asked to memorize too many words.

# CHAPTER 4
# THIRD SUNDAY IN LENT: PROMISED GUIDANCE

## Gathering Music: "How Great Thou Art"

Taryn Harbridge's instrumental arrangement
https://youtu.be/lsigbU596d4

## Centering Words

Dance before God. It is a joyous thing to fulfill the law of the LORD.

## Lighting the Christ Candle

*As you light the Christ candle on your altar, give thanks for the promise of God's guidance. Invite the light of Christ to revive your soul, as you allow the law of God to bring wisdom and joy to your life.*

# Memory Verse: Psalm 19:7, 10a NIV

The law of the LORD is perfect,
   refreshing the soul.
The statutes of the LORD are trustworthy,
   making wise the simple.
They are more precious than gold.

# Opening Prayer

Speak once more, O God,
   of the ways of life and death.
For your law is perfect,
   reviving the soul.
Your commandments are trustworthy,
   saving the ignorant from folly.
Guide me each and every day,
   that I might worship you
      in spirit and in truth. Amen.

# Songs

**"Spirit, Spirit of Gentleness"**
Kristen Young as soloist with ensemble, guitar and lyrics
https://youtu.be/TcxLeObxoJs

Golden Ears United Church's soloist and piano with lyrics
https://youtu.be/9q0ydibNHcs

Mary Munson piano and flute arrangement with lyrics (no vocals)
https://youtu.be/iwIZJpCCBIM

*–OR–*

**"Oceans" ("Where Feet May Fail")**
Hillsong UNITED (lyric video)
https://youtu.be/dy9nwe9_xzw

ELENYI Music (cover vocal performance with cello and piano)
https://youtu.be/ssBmFi51z_k

# Scripture Reading:
# Exodus 20:2-5a, 7a, 8-10a, 12-17

I am the LORD your God who brought you out of Egypt, out of the
house of slavery.

You must have no other gods before me.

Do not make an idol for yourself . . . of anything in the sky above or on
the earth below or in the waters under the earth. Do not bow down
to them or worship them.

Do not use the LORD your God's name as if it were of no significance.

Remember the Sabbath day and treat it as holy. Six days you may work
and do all your tasks, but the seventh day is a Sabbath to the LORD
your God.

Honor your father and your mother so that your life will be long on the
fertile land that the LORD your God is giving you.

Do not kill.

Do not commit adultery.

Do not steal.

Do not testify falsely against your neighbor.

Do not desire and try to take . . . anything . . . that belongs to your
neighbor.

# Meditation

Having chosen to effect salvation history by working through one family
and the nations Abraham and Sarah birthed, God gave this fledgling people
the Ten Commandments. Known as the decalogue, these commandments
form the backbone of all three Abrahamic faiths: Judaism, Christianity, and
Islam. While the first five commandments pronounce how to honor God
and your parents, the last five commandments place restraints on human
behavior. Such commandments would not have been necessary if the chosen
people had already been honoring God and their parents, or if they had not
been lying, stealing, killing, coveting, bearing false witness, and committing
adultery. Yet, these commandments were never meant to be a burden. Indeed,
the rabbis speak of the joy of fulfilling each of the 613 mitvot or commandments in the Hebrew Bible, not just the ten listed in the decalogue. Following

God's instructions unveils new freedoms and joys, as you find the fulfillment and satisfaction that comes with aligning yourself with God's purposes for your life. Which commandment do you have the most difficulty following? Which commandment gives you the greatest strength and hope? Lent is an auspicious time to work on being a faithful follower. And with the rabbis, it can be a joyful time indeed.

## Response to the Word

*Write a journal entry or do a self-guided meditation on God's command-ments and precepts. Imagine them as protective boundaries and guard-rails to keep you safe from self-injury and the pain of regret. Envision the law of God as a blanket of love, warming you against the cold watches of the night when fears and anxieties lead to actions that tear your soul. Express gratitude for this loving protection and be joyful every time you fulfill the precepts of God.*

## Song: "Take Time to Be Holy"

Dallas Christian Adult Concert Choir (a capella choir with lyrics)
https://youtu.be/rFApbg-wcmE

Teri Elmore lyric video (David and Steven Au's folk-style vocal & instrumental ensemble)
https://youtu.be/WblkcQYxdp8

Mormon Tabernacle Choir (alternative melody)
https://youtu.be/eYLpkRT5Nzw

## Blessing

Dance before God.
Following God's commandments fills the soul with joy.
From the folly of ignorance,
God offers the promise of guidance—
guidance in the ways of life.

# Sending Activities

*Choose an activity or find your own action of commitment to follow God's guidance in the week ahead.*

- Add to your Lenten sacred space/worship altar or art project by drawing, painting, sculpting, or gathering an item that reminds you of God's loving guidance.

- With children, draw and decorate a directional arrow or compass together or "side by side" on FaceTime or Zoom. After you've completed the craft, offer a simple prayer for God to be your compass and guide.

- Read two verses of Psalm 19's fourteen verses each day over the course of the week. Read slowly, aloud if you are comfortable. If you want to practice *lectio divina*, add these steps to your scripture reading practice each day.

  - *Pray.* Have a loving conversation with God.

  - *Meditate.* Reflect deeply on the text. Listen to what your spirit and God's Spirit may be saying to you in these verses.

  - *Contemplate.* Rest in God's presence.

  - *Act.* Respond to the passage as you sense God's guidance.

- Send today's memory verse or a favorite scripture to family, friends, church members or church staff. Include a word of appreciation for the way in which they are also precious to you, like silver or gold.

- Anonymously deliver small gift cards (for a local grocery story or small business) to a few neighbors this week. Reflect on how much better it feels to give than it does to covet.

- Reflect on an Ash Wednesday or Lenten commitment you made. Is the commitment helping you draw closer to God's promises? Why or why not?

- Recite today's memory verse each day this week. Use whichever memory technique works best for you: memorize small phrases at a time until you know the entire verse; write the verse on a Post-it note, placing it where you can see and recite it several times each day; imagine a visual for the verse's meaning; or paraphrase the verse and memorize this paraphrase. If memorizing with small children, give them a short phrase before adding additional phrases. Some small children are better at memory work than adults, while others become frustrated if asked to memorize too many words.

# CHAPTER 5
# FOURTH SUNDAY
# IN LENT:
# PROMISE OF THE HEART

## Gathering Music

**"Near to the Heart of God"**
Linda Coetzee (piano arrangement)
https://youtu.be/OdCx7W4dc5Q

*–OR–*

**"Here's My Heart"**
Passion Music (with David Crowder)
https://youtu.be/cvl-MfqvgkE

## Centering Words

God has written the law of love on your heart. Practice discernment of this love and you will live.

# Lighting the Christ Candle

*As you light the Christ candle on your altar, give thanks for God's promise of the heart. Invite the light of Christ into your heart. Allow it to illumine the law of God written there. Sit with the awareness that you must practice this law each and every day if it is to guide you as God intends.*

# Memory Verse: Jeremiah 31:33b, Adapted

I will put my law within them
    and engrave it on their hearts.
I will be their God,
    and they will be my people.

# Opening Prayer

Engraver of the human heart,
    your law of love strives to burst forth
        with every beat of my heart.
Work within me this day,
    that the majesty of your love
        may shine in the words I speak
        and radiate in the actions I take.
    Amen.

# Song: "O Love That Wilt Not Let Me Go"

Celebration Choir, orchestra, and lyrics
https://youtu.be/nt69WDtYNLo

20schemes Music guitar, vocals, and lyrics
https://youtu.be/xJOUtCModPI

Fountainview Academy a capella ensemble
https://youtu.be/TvA6PYa54sg

# Scripture Reading: Jeremiah 31:31-33, Adapted

The time is coming, declares the LORD,
  when I will make a new covenant
  with the people of Israel and Judah.
It won't be like the covenant I made with their ancestors
  when I took them by the hand
  to lead them out of the land of Egypt.
They broke that covenant with me
  even though I was their husband, declares the LORD.
No, this is the covenant that I will make
  with the people of Israel after that time,
    declares the LORD.
I will put my law within them
  and engrave it on their hearts.
I will be their God,
  and they will be my people.

# Meditation

While the Ten Commandments were a huge advancement toward building good and godly communities, individual human behavior continued to fall short. Realizing that commandments written on tablets of stone would not keep the house of Israel in the ways that leads to life, God promised to make a new covenant with the people: God would put the law within them and write it on their very hearts. If people would look within, they could learn to discern the instructions written there. Such discernment is not easy. It takes patience and practice: in prayer, in meditation, in study, and in works of mercy and compassion. But as you learn to discern the law God has written on your heart, you will learn how to live as love in the world, and you will discover how to fully embrace what it means to love God, neighbor, and self with all your heart, soul, mind, and strength. Let this Lenten season be a time of learning to read what God has written within.

# Music for Reflection

**"Change My Heart, O God"**
Easy Worship Resources video of potter with vocal ensemble, guitar, and lyrics
https://youtu.be/IlSmG-_eJTU

*–OR–*

**"Heart of the Matter"**
India Arie (R & B style with lyrics)
https://youtu.be/7AOBhmUVGDQ

Madeline Merle (acoustic recording)
https://youtu.be/o_0-dai54E0

# Response to the Word

*Silently watch the potter casting the pot in "Change My Heart" or reflect on the words of "Heart of the Matter" as you listen to one of the videos above. Where you are yearning for God to re-mold, re-shape, or even break down and recreate your life anew? To truly create your heart anew, reflect on people you need to forgive or from whom you need to seek forgiveness. Invite God to be the potter who will enact such change and write God's very presence on your heart and soul.*

# Closing Song

**"Here I Am, Lord"**
Pastor Madeline's lyric video (Chris Bray's recording)
https://youtu.be/4t6mz8yoocY

White Chapel UMC choir and orchestra (no lyrics)
https://youtu.be/_UkTlj2uPl4

Truth According to Scripture (choir, Orchestra, and lyrics)
https://youtu.be/m5wfvGqPNHE

*–OR–*

**"Write Your Story"**
Fancesca Battistelli—SMN's lyric video with Battistelli's recording
https://youtu.be/eKcImiTxqKg

# Blessing

With God's law of love engraved on your heart,
   let this inner compass guide you.
Discern the still small voice
   that whispers with every heartbeat.
From cold words written on a page,
   discover the promise of the heart—
   the warm beat of the living law of love.

# Sending Activities

*Choose an activity or find your own way to express God's love and law written on your heart and offered in love to the world.*

- Add to your Lenten sacred space/worship altar or art project by drawing, painting, sculpting, or gathering an item that that symbolizes a changed heart—a heart dedicated to God and God's law of love.

- With children, choose another heart craft you can do together or "side by side" on FaceTime or Zoom. Or pull out your Ash Wednesday craft and see if anyone wants to change it, add to it, or decorate it more fully. Listen to one or two of the songs above as you work together on your "changed hearts."

- Purchase a heart-shaped card or print a heart on blank note-paper with the words: "God's heart is in your heart." Post this card or note where you can view it each day as a reminder of this week's theme. You may purchase or print additional copies to send to family and friends, or church members and staff, as a word of encouragement. You might even include the scripture reference, Jeremiah 31:31-34.

- Send a note of apology to someone you may have hurt or wronged. When you mail the letter, breathe in the peace that arises from forgiving yourself, allowing God's love to fill your heart and leave its imprint on your life.

- Journal or write a note to yourself that offers grace and forgiveness for past regrets, making room for God's love to fill your heart and leave its imprint on your life.

- Support a non-profit that is receiving gifts and ask them what donations they most need. Post the need on your social media site, encouraging people to donate. If you are able, collect local donations and deliver them where they are needed most.

- Reflect on an Ash Wednesday or Lenten commitment you made. Is the commitment helping you draw closer to God's love? Why or why not?

- Recite today's memory verse each day this week. Use whichever memory technique works best for you: memorize small phrases at a time until you know the entire verse; write the verse on a Post-it note, placing it where you can see and recite it several times each day; imagine a visual for the verse's meaning; or paraphrase the verse and memorize this paraphrase. If memorizing with small children, give them a short phrase before adding additional phrases. Some small children are better at memory work than adults, while others become frustrated if asked to memorize too many words.

- Alternately to the memory verse, invite children to learn the Ten Commandments with you this week. Here are several fun ways to do this with children:

    ○ http://www.myblessedhome.net/2009/11/fun-way-to-memorize-the-ten-commandments/

    ○ https://www.youtube.com/watch?v=8pBrw4uVgz8&feature=emb_logo

    ○ https://youtu.be/kYHzN9wswck

# CHAPTER 6
# FIFTH SUNDAY IN LENT: THE PROMISE OF GRACE

## Gathering Music: "Amazing Grace"

Ian Mulder piano & London Symphony Orchestra (instrumental arrangement with images)
https://youtu.be/H4GWkTU41wk

Gospel Music Powerpoint (violin and piano arrangement with lyrics)
https://youtu.be/h82qwHNOcq8

Rosemary Siemen (vocal, violin, and piano arrangement)
https://youtu.be/rxuSdBDib-s

## Centering Words

God so loved the world. . . . This love is all you need—all you will ever need. Take it. This love can save the world.

## Lighting the Christ Candle

*As you light the Christ candle on your altar, give thanks for the promise of God's grace. Invite the light of Christ's love to fill you with the love that God sent to save the world.*

# Memory Verse: John 3:16

God so loved the world that he gave his only Son,
    so that everyone who believes in him won't perish
    but will have eternal life.

# Opening Prayer

God of immeasurable grace,
    you sent your Son into the world
        in an act of love so great,
            it is hard to comprehend.
Fashion your servant into a vessel
    of your love and light,
        that I may be worthy of the one
            who came to save us all. Amen.

# Song:
# "There's a Wideness in God's Mercy"

John Wesley Slider's lyric video (choir, organ and lyrics)
https://www.youtube.com/watch?v=XcgwTbi4ka4&t=2s

Riverside Church (virtual choir, organ and lyrics)
https://youtu.be/LfyZIJUHKpU

# Scripture Reading: John 3:16-17;
# Ephesians 2:4b-8 NIV

God so loved the world that he gave his one and only Son, that whoever believes in him shall not perish but have eternal life. For God did not send his Son into the world to condemn the world, but to save the world through him.

God, who is rich in mercy, made us alive with Christ even when we were dead in transgressions—it is by grace you have been saved. And God raised us up with Christ and seated us with him in the heavenly realms in Christ Jesus, in order that in the coming ages he might show the incomparable riches of his grace, expressed in his kindness to us in Christ Jesus.

# Poem

Love is much more outrageous than you can imagine.
It runs naked in the streets shouting your name.
It wants everyone to know
you have been promised to the Beloved.

Love is so beautiful it will make you gasp
when you finally see the radiance of God's glowing heart,
see nothing separates you but the sheerest veil,
choose daily to fling it wide.

> —Tina Datsko de Sánchez, "Love is much more outrageous than
> you can imagine." Used by permission of author. Forthcoming in a
> book by Pilgrim Press.

# Meditation

Abraham and Sarah's offspring had failed to be the blessing and light to the
nations God intended them to be. Even writing the law of God on human
hearts failed to bring God's kingdom to earth as it was in heaven. Humanity
needed a course correction, and dramatic action was required. The prologue
of John's Gospel (chapter 1) is more than a third creation story—a story de-
claring that everything that exists came into being through the Word—it in-
troduces the culmination of salvation history made explicit in John 3:16-17.
God sent the Word into the world, not to condemn it, but to save it. God
not only upped the ante, God went all in. But does the world want to be
saved? There is an iconic scene in Pixar's movie, *The Incredibles*, when Oliver
Sansweet's lawyer protests the foiling of his client's suicide: "Mr. Sansweet
didn't ask to be saved. Mr. Sansweet didn't want to be saved. And the inju-
ries received from Mr. Incredible's so-called 'actions' cause him daily pain."
"Hey, I saved your life!" Mr. Incredible objects. "You didn't save my life, you
ruined my death," Oliver Sansweet shouts back. When all hope seems lost,
do you want to be saved? Do you even think you are worth saving? God
thinks we are all worth saving. That's the message of grace. The Word comes
to you in grace and mercy when your soul cries out in anguish, and the Spirit
intercedes with sighs too deep for words. This grace is freely given. All you

have to do is sink into it, rest in it, and allow it to fill you and heal you. This is harder than it sounds, for it will mean living with daily pain. But it will also mean embracing daily joy, love, and hope for the future. And ultimately, it will bring the blessing of peace. This is good news indeed.

## Response to the Word

*"When all hope seems lost, do you want to be saved? Do you even think you are worth saving?" Reflect on these questions silently, in your journal, or in conversations with friends. Following this reflection, listen to your favorite musical selection from today's service. As you listen, breathe slowly and deeply, inviting grace to fill each breath. Close this time by praying for grace to fill your days, giving thanks to God for this glorious gift.*

## Song: "To God Be the Glory"

Royal Albert Hall Choir (with lyrics)
https://youtu.be/-15v9iworAU

Roar VBS Children's Choir (with lyrics)
https://youtu.be/Y0dQbfbSW0Q

Andrae Crouch and All Star Choir Tribute
https://youtu.be/0RZTYDPavEY

## Blessing

God's love fills the world.
Let this love fill you.
Let it move in and through you.
From the darkness of death,
God offers the light of salvation—
the incomparable riches of Christ's grace.

# Sending Activities

*Choose an activity or find your own way to share God's grace with others and with yourself in the week ahead.*

- Add to your Lenten sacred space/worship altar or art project by drawing, painting, sculpting, or gathering an item that that symbolizes the mysterious gift of grace.

- With children, invite them to write down or dictate their own table grace prayer. Help them if necessary, but encourage them come up with their own words. Talk about why this prayer of blessing might be called a grace. There are no right or wrong answers, so just listen openly and see what you and the children discover together about prayer and grace as you talk. After your conversation, invite them to say their prayer aloud and encourage them to offer that prayer before upcoming meals throughout the season.

- When speaking with people this week and even when thinking about and talking to yourself, pay attention to the words you choose and use. Focus on words that are kind and gentle. Even if you correct yourself or others, find a way to gently say what needs to be said. This gift of grace can transform a conversation and even perhaps a relationship.

- Think of a friend or neighbor in need of help or support. Surprise them with an anonymous gift on their front porch: a bag of basic essentials, a grocery store gift card, a stuffed animal, or a backpack full of school supplies.

- Share the Roar VBS video (https://youtu.be/Y0dQbfbSW0Q) with children in your household. Decide together if they would like to learn the movements. If so, learn them together and enjoy dancing and singing as a family. Alternately, offer the same opportunity via video conference or safely distanced in your backyard with grandchildren or the children of friends who might enjoy another adult spending some time with their children.

- Reflect on an Ash Wednesday or Lenten commitment you made. Is the commitment helping you lean more fully into God's grace? Why or why not?

- Recite today's memory verse each day this week. Use whichever memory technique works best for you: memorize small phrases at a time until you know the entire verse; write the verse on a Post-it note, placing it where you can see and recite it several times each day; imagine a visual for the verse's meaning; or paraphrase the verse and memorize this paraphrase. If memorizing with small children, give them a short phrase before adding additional phrases. Some small children are better at memory work than adults, while others become frustrated if asked to memorize too many words.

# CHAPTER 7
# PALM SUNDAY: THE PROMISED KING

## Gathering Music: "The Palms" (Faure)

Instrumental (piano and cello)
https://youtu.be/ARHOb9TLrK0

Crystal Cathedral Choir (orchestra and lyrics)
https://youtu.be/Etrgxd6fSvc

## Centering Words

This is a day of exaltation and joy, as Jesus arrives in Jerusalem to loud hosannas. Still, winds portend a coming storm in the week ahead. Now is the time to follow Jesus.

## Lighting the Christ Candle

*As you light the Christ candle on your altar, give thanks for God's promised King. Invite the light of Christ to fill you with the joy of that first Palm Sunday, when children sang their hosannas to the one who came in the name of the Lord. In preparation for today's celebration, you may want to find a leafy branch to raise and wave during the songs. If worshiping with children, gather multiple branches so each child has several to celebrate with.*

# Memory Verse: Psalm 118:1 NIV, adapted

Give thanks to the LORD, for he is good;
God's steadfast love endures forever.

# Opening Prayer

I give you thanks, O God, for you are good;
your steadfast love endures forever.
Open my mouth to shout hosannas
to the one who came in the name of the Lord.
Open my lips to laugh with the children
on this Palm Sunday celebration,
even as we remember the events to come.
Amen.

# Song: "Hosanna, Loud Hosanna"

First UMC of Houston (organ, quartet, and lyrics)
https://youtu.be/M_pWJg5N_ZQ

Visalia CRC (acoustic version with guitar, percussion, vocalist and lyrics)
https://youtu.be/AuB5qRvO1QA

# Scripture Reading: Mark 11:1-4, 7-10

When Jesus and his followers approached Jerusalem, they came to Bethphage and Bethany at the Mount of Olives. Jesus gave two disciples a task, saying to them, "Go into the village over there. As soon as you enter it, you will find tied up there a colt that no one has ridden. Untie it and bring it here. If anyone says to you, 'Why are you doing this?' say, 'Its master needs it, and he will send it back right away.'"

They brought the colt to Jesus and threw their clothes upon it, and he sat on it. Many people spread out their clothes on the road while others spread branches cut from the fields. Those in front of him and those following were shouting, "Hosanna! Blessings on the one who comes in the name of the Lord! Blessings on the coming kingdom of our ancestor David! Hosanna in the highest!"

# Meditation

Palm Sunday is a hard day to celebrate. It's hard to watch the Word made flesh, the very light of the world, being welcomed into the holy city with shouts of Hosanna, with waving palms and scattered garments, all the while knowing how this story ends. "The light came to his own people, and his own people didn't welcome him" (John 1:11). Or they did until they didn't. Children sang and danced on this day. Parents dreamed of what the coming kingdom of their ancestor David would mean for the downfall of Rome's occupation. All would be well as long as Jesus acted like the king they wanted him to be, the king they needed him to be. But alas, our welcome can be short-lived when guests disappoint us. The people should have known better. What kind of king comes riding into Jerusalem on a lowly donkey and not on a majestic horse? What sort of king says "Blessed are the pure of heart, for they will see God" (Luke 5:8 NIV)? What kind of king looks to children as examples of how to enter his kingdom? There's a reason churches do Palm Sunday processions with their children and youth. It's not too late to reclaim the child-like joy and welcome of this day. It's not too late to welcome the light of the world anew into your heart.

# Response to the Word

*Gaze at the lighted Christ candle or at a favorite artistic image of Christ. (You can always find one online.) Give Christ thanks for arriving in your life, in our world, not merely on that Jerusalem day of celebration long ago. Offer the Christ-image an appreciative smile. If you're brave enough, wave a leafy branch and shout aloud, "Hosanna in the highest! Blessed are you who comes in the name of the Lord!" Shout it over and over, allowing your smile to become a big belly laugh of joy. If you need help laughing, check out this World Laughter Day special video: https:// youtu.be/qrQqLLnW7ok.*

38

# Song: "I Danced in the Morning" ("Lord of the Dance")

First-Plymouth Church Lincoln (choir, congregation, organ and lyrics)
https://youtu.be/Xkk0YodJqH8

Franklyn Schaefer (contemporary version with lyrics)
https://youtu.be/214Vdyo6kSs

Gaither TV (a capella rendition—no lyrics)
https://youtu.be/ZsRE37jpUOw

# Blessing

On the back of a donkey,
    Jesus came to bless me.
With a love that did not count the cost,
    Jesus came to heal me.
With the power of the Holy Spirit,
    Jesus came to save me.
From hopelessness and despair,
    Jesus came to fulfill God's promise
    of the coming King.

# Sending Activities

*Choose an activity or find your own way to celebrate Christ's presence with others and with yourself in the week ahead.*

- Add a leafy branch (palm, fern, etc.), palm frond, or drawing to your Lenten sacred space/worship altar or art project.

- If you are worshiping at home with children, invite them to gather leafy branches from the yard. Or have them draw, color, and cut out their own. Tape their drawing to sticks or rulers, then host a palm parade with your children. March around your home or neighborhood, laughing, singing, or simply telling each other stories of Jesus.

- Before or after worship today, if you have access to palm or fern fronds, deliver them to church members who are not able to attend church in person. If safety requires "contact-less" deliver, simply ring the doorbell and drop the fronds on their front porches with a note, "A Holy Week gift from your church family."

- Reflect on an Ash Wednesday or Lenten commitment you made. Is the commitment helping you experience Christ's presence? Why or why not?

- Recite today's memory verse each day this week. Use whichever memory technique works best for you: memorize small phrases at a time until you know the entire verse; write the verse on a Post-it note, placing it where you can see and recite it several times each day; imagine a visual for the verse's meaning; or paraphrase the verse and memorize this paraphrase. If memorizing with small children, give them a short phrase before adding additional phrases. Some small children are better at memory work than adults, while others become frustrated if asked to memorize too many words.

# CHAPTER 8
# HOLY THURSDAY: THE PROMISE OF LOVE

## Gathering Music

**"O Jesus, I Have Promised"**
Adam Couchman's piano arrangement
https://youtu.be/1fta5ZEE5sg

*–OR–*

**"They'll Know We Are Christians"**
Piano Brothers's piano arrangement
https://youtu.be/GnRGyoIwBNE

## Centering Words

The promise of Love calls. They will know we are Christians by our love.

## Lighting the Christ Candle

*As you light the Christ candle on your altar, give thanks for the promise of God's love. Invite the light of Christ to fill you with this love—the love you have received from Christ, the love Christ asks you to share with others.*

# Memory Verse: John 13:34, Adapted

"I give you a new commandment: Love one another.
Just as I have loved you,
  so you also must love one another."

# Opening Prayer

Servant God, be with me *us*
  in the celebration and remembrance
    of Christ's Passover meal with his disciples.
Be present in the breaking of the bread,
  in the sharing of the cup,
    and in the very act of remembering.
Grant me a humble heart and willing spirit,*s*
  that I may serve others with the same love *we*
    that I am loved by you. Amen. *we*

# Song

**"What Wondrous Love Is This"**
St. Olaf Choir (a capella)
https://youtu.be/DsVnvN3EVxY

Chelsea Moon with the Franz Brothers (piano, guitar, and soloist)
https://youtu.be/1g26dbNJYJI

St. Columba's Episcopal Church (virtual choir with organ and lyrics)
https://youtu.be/6dga05WAkqQ

–OR–

**"O Love, How Deep, How Broad, How High"**
Lorenz's Lloyd Larsen arrangement, choir, piano, and violin
https://youtu.be/ZkVGKJUd64E

Szabo Music (lyrics, piano, and soloist)
https://youtu.be/0EXzSpq9v44

# Scripture Reading: John 13:34-35, Adapted

"I give you a new commandment: Love one another. Just as I have loved you, so you also must love one another. This is how everyone will know that you are my disciples, when you love each other."

# Meditation

Never underestimate the power of memory. Jews share the Passover meal each year to remember how the destroyer passed over the Israelite's houses, sparing the lives of their first-born, when the Lord smote the land of Egypt on the eve of the Exodus. Shared remembrances bring strength and endurance during times of trial. Jesus knew his disciples needed such strength and endurance if they were to face the days ahead, so he gathered them to celebrate Passover and forever transformed the meaning of this holy festival for his followers. The bread he offers is his body, the bread of life. The cup he shares is his love poured out for you and for many, the cup of salvation. This remembrance of him is a remembrance of love, of strength for the journey. When you eat and drink in Jesus's name, you are remembering the incarnate love that came down to save the world. Jesus's commandment to love in today's scripture flows inescapably from the self-giving of Love itself. Remember this love today and always. Never underestimate the power of memory.

# Remembrance of the Lord's Supper

*To prepare, have a piece of bread on a plate or paten, and wine or grape juice in a cup or chalice. If worshiping with children, invite them to help you prepare the bread and juice. Children may be more comfortable with simpler wording.*

Eat the bread of life,
  and drink the wine of forgiveness.
Taste the promise of grace,
  the promise of Christ's Love.

*Take the bread in your hands, and forming the shape of a rice bowl before your heart, meditate on Christ's word's:*

"Take, eat; this is my body which is given for you.
  Do this in remembrance of me."

*When you feel ready, take and eat, giving thanks for the bread of heaven that Christ offers to strengthen you for the journey. Then take the cup or chalice, and holding it before your heart, meditate on Christ's word's:*

"Drink from this, all of you;
  this is my life in the new covenant,
  poured out for you and for many,
  for the forgiveness of sins.
Do this, as often as you drink it,
  in remembrance of me."

*When you feel ready, take and drink, giving thanks for the cup of salvation that nourishes your spirit through the power of God's Holy Spirit.*

# Song

**"In Remembrance of Me"** (Ragan and Red)
The St. Paul Inspirit Ensemble
https://youtu.be/sCUfTx8dzE4

Robert Kochis's solo with lyrics
https://youtu.be/nV_kFlsKrQU

*–OR–*

**"I Will Remember You"**
Sarah McLachlan (Adam Soja's video with rolling images)
https://youtu.be/FacDkraAvlI

Sarah McLachlan (The Forgotten Dawn's video with lyrics)
https://youtu.be/XQtAOuBjysc

# Blessing

Blessed by God, you are called to live.
Fed by Christ, you are called to serve.
From the cycle of hatred and violence,
 God offers the promise of Love—
 the promise of a godly future.
They will know we are Christians by our love.

# Sending Activities

*Choose an activity or find your own way to share God's love with others in the week ahead.*

- Add to your Lenten sacred space/worship altar or art project a communion symbol (cup, plate, bread, grapes) to symbolize the remembrance of Jesus's great love.

- Send love notes to people who are particularly important in your life, expressing how much you love and appreciate them. Offer them help as a token of your love.

- If it is safe to do so, offer to drive a friend to a doctor's appointment or take their child to a local park. Or simply call and ask how they are doing, listening deeply to what is going on in their life right now.

- Donate to your church, your favorite charity, or a struggling neighborhood family.

- Remember your Ash Wednesday or Lenten commitments and simply give thanks for the blessings they have brought.

- Recite today's memory verse daily throughout the week ahead. Memorize it or post it where you can see it each day as a reminder of Christ's call to love one another as he has loved us.

# CHAPTER 9
# GOOD FRIDAY: LIFTED UP BY THE PROMISE

## Gathering Music: "Were You There When They Crucified My Lord?"

Tatiana (vocal arrangement with scenes from *The Passion of the Christ*)
https://youtu.be/MPmGcridHQ8

## Centering Words

Were you there when they crucified my Lord?
Were you the betrayal in Judas's kiss?
Were you the faithlessness in Peter's denial?
Were you the hatred in the crowd?
Were you the indifference in Pilate's heart?
Were you the silence . . . when no bird sang?

## Shrouding the Christ Candle

*Take a piece of black cloth and cover the unlit Christ candle, for on Good Friday, the Light of the World is witnessed leaving the world.*

# Memory Verse: Isaiah 52:13 NIV

See, my servant will act wisely;
  he will be raised and lifted up and highly exalted.

# Opening Prayer

Where do you go, Elusive One,
  when all hope fades?
Where were you when your own Son,
  dying on a cross, cried out with the psalmist:
    "My God, my God,
      why have you forsaken me?"
Your ways are inscrutable,
  shrouded in mystery.
The emptiness of your absence is terrifying.
Stay with me in my hour of need,
  and do not abandon me when I deny you.
Amen.

# Song: "Stay with Me"

Marcos Pardo (Taizé choir and orchestra with English and Spanish lyrics)
https://youtu.be/r63EqwUp-7Y

# Scripture Reading:
# Isaiah 52:13; 53:1, 3-6 NIV

See, my servant will act wisely;
  he will be raised and lifted up and highly exalted.
Who has believed our message
  and to whom has the arm of the LORD been revealed?
He was despised and rejected by mankind,
  a man of suffering, and familiar with pain.
Like one from whom people hide their faces
  he was despised, and we held him in low esteem.

Surely he took up our pain
    and bore our suffering,
yet we considered him punished by God,
    stricken by him, and afflicted.
But he was pierced for our transgressions,
    he was crushed for our iniquities;
the punishment that brought us peace was on him,
    and by his wounds we are healed.
We all, like sheep, have gone astray,
    each of us has turned to our own way;
and the LORD has laid on him
    the iniquity of us all.

# Meditation

Christians confess Isaiah's Suffering Servant as none other than Christ Jesus. One who was thought abandoned and smitten by God was pierced for our transgressions. By his wounds we are healed. Through his tribulation we find peace. How did salvation history seemingly take such a strange and unlikely turn? How could the day of Jesus's death be called Good Friday? Isaiah says God's servant will be raised and lifted up and highly exalted. When the Word made flesh was lifted up on the cross at Golgotha, God highly exalted him. The Word made flesh, who came from above, was lifted up that we might be lifted with him. When Jesus tells Nicodemus he must be born again in John 3:3, the Greek word for *again* also means from above. When you cry out with the psalmist, "My strength is dried up like a piece of broken pottery. You've set me down in the dust of death" (Psalm 22:15), know that Christ is here to lift you up. This is a day to truly be born from above, to stand and be counted with those who live in the light, to journey with those who dwell secure in the inscrutable mysteries of God.

# Response to the Word:
# Psalm 22:14-15, Adapted

*Reflect on these words from the psalmist. Read them several times and allow the images to enlighten your mind, fill your heart, and sink into your very bones.*

I'm poured out like water.
My heart is like wax;
    it melts inside me.
My strength is dried up
    like a piece of broken pottery.
You've set me down in the dust of death.

*If you have been doing the Ash Wednesday activity (giving up something that saps your strength and makes your spirit feel like a piece of broken pottery), lift up your burden to Christ one last time, knowing that the one who was lifted up on a cross at Golgatha can release you from its weight once and for all. If you have not been doing the Ash Wednesday activity, or if you simply want to do something new on Good Friday, write down on a small scrap of paper something that lies fallow in your life that you would like to see burst forth with new life this Easter Sunday. Fold the paper and cover it on your altar so that it hides out of sight. Spend the next three days in the emptiness of the tomb, waiting and praying for a sign that Christ, who was lifted up and glorified on Good Friday, can lift up your hopes and dreams.*

# Sending Song

**"When I Survey the Wondrous Cross"**
Fountainview Academy (orchestra and vocals)
https://youtu.be/9DHszgAVFdw

The Mark Thallander Foundation Festival Choir (arr. Martin for orchestra, organ and choir)
https://youtu.be/fEOLUnoQdmQ

Fernando Ortega (vocal arrangement with lyrics)
https://youtu.be/Tkx8WAycYAc

*–OR–*

**"Wondrous Cross"**
Chris Tomlin (contemporary Christian arrangement with lyrics)
https://youtu.be/qGlUdgrvJgo

# Sending Activities

*Choose an activity or find your own way to share God's love with others in the week ahead.*

- Add a black piece of cloth or a simple cross to your Lenten sacred space/worship altar or art project in remembrance of Jesus's death.

- Spend the next two days as quietly as possible, reflecting on Jesus's death and his time in the tomb. Allow the quiet and emptiness of waiting to prepare your heart and mind to receive and celebrate the miracle of resurrection on Sunday.

- With children or other family members, decorate Easter eggs (or stuff plastic eggs) with symbols that remind your family of Holy Week, Jesus, and resurrection.

- Reflect on an Ash Wednesday or Lenten commitment you have. Do you want to carry this commitment, as is or modified, into the Easter season? Or do you want to let it go completely? Honor what is best for your spiritual journey, as you rest in the tomb with Jesus over the next few days, and prepare your heart to celebrate the resurrection in the season ahead.

CPSIA information can be obtained
at www.ICGtesting.com
Printed in the USA
LVHW042158140121
676517LV00004B/4